Style and Swing

Style and Swing

12 Structured Handbags for Beginners and Beyond

SUSAN DUNLOP

Martingale®
Create with Confidence

DEDICATION

To my mum, Annemarie, and dad, Myles; my husband, Allan;
and my children, Stefan, Kyle, James, and Christopher.
Thank you for all your support and encouragement.

Style and Swing: 12 Structured Handbags
for Beginners and Beyond
© 2015 by Susan Dunlop

Martingale®
19021 120th Ave. NE, Ste. 102
Bothell, WA 98011-9511 USA
ShopMartingale.com

Printed in China
20 19 18 17 16 15   8 7 6 5 4 3 2 1

**Library of Congress Cataloging-in-Publication Data
is available upon request.**

ISBN: 978-1-60468-467-4

33614056402505

MISSION STATEMENT

*Dedicated to providing quality products and service
to inspire creativity.*

CREDITS

PUBLISHER AND CHIEF VISIONARY OFFICER
Jennifer Erbe Keltner

EDITORIAL DIRECTOR
Karen Costello Soltys

ACQUISITIONS EDITOR
Karen M. Burns

TECHNICAL EDITOR
Rebecca Kemp Brent

COPY EDITOR
Marcy Heffernan

DESIGN DIRECTOR
Paula Schlosser

PHOTOGRAPHER
Brent Kane

PRODUCTION MANAGER
Regina Girard

COVER AND
INTERIOR DESIGNER
Adrienne Smitke

ILLUSTRATOR
Christine Erikson

Contents

Introduction

I love sewing. I'm addicted to vibrant fabrics, and I love making bags and accessories. I am very lucky to have grown up among a crafting family that likes to knit, crochet, sew, paint, embroider, make felt . . . I could go on. It was inevitable that I would catch the crafting bug too. Although I didn't get into sewing until much later in life, it very quickly became my favorite pastime. I get so much enjoyment from sewing up my own designs—and I love to inspire others too! This is what prompted me to become a project designer and eventually led me to writing this book.

I've designed the projects with all levels of sewing ability in mind. If you're new to sewing or you've never tried bag making before, you'll find a simple but very elegant handbag suitable for beginners. This project shows that even the simplest of designs can really stand out in modern, vibrant fabrics. As you work your way through the book, each project becomes a bit more complex, building your confidence and skill level. If you're an experienced sewist, jump ahead to whatever project strikes your fancy. There's a good mix of advanced-beginner as well as intermediate-level projects to choose from and to stick your pins into. I've also included some useful information on the tools you'll need, fabric preparation, interfacings, sewing terms, and a comprehensive how-to techniques section.

I'm so happy to share my ideas with you, and I look forward to seeing what you come up with. I'm always so pleased to see how someone has adapted a design to suit his or her needs—an extra pocket, a different handle, clever use of recycled fabrics, or unique embellishments. That's what I love so much about bag making: the possibilities are endless, the projects are customizable, and you can truly make any bag design your own.

Happy sewing,

~Susan

Recommended Equipment and Tools

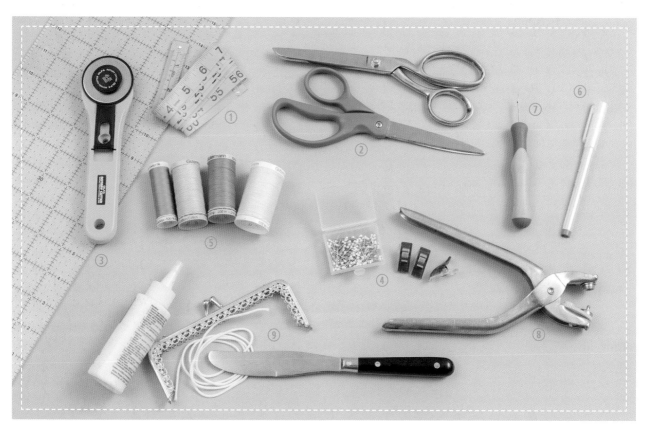

A selection of equipment required for making bags and accessories

You'll find all the tools that I've used for the projects in this book listed here; some are essential and some are suggestions to make life easier. You don't need to spend a fortune, but for some items I recommend buying the best that you can comfortably afford, for quality and durability.

Tape measure and ruler. A flexible tape measure is useful during project construction, and a nonflexible ruler is needed for measuring the fabric pieces as you cut. ①

Scissors. A pair of dressmaking shears is essential for fabric cutting. I recommend buying the best you can afford and using them only for fabric to keep them sharp and in good condition. You'll also need some general-purpose scissors for other cutting jobs. ②

Rotary cutter, ruler, and self-healing cutting mat. Rotary cutters are available in a range of different blade sizes, with 45 mm being the standard. Along with a quilter's acrylic ruler and a self-healing cutting mat, rotary cutters make cutting fabric very quick and easy. A 6" x 18" ruler is a good size to use along with an 18" x 24" or 12" x 18" (A2 or A3) cutting mat. ③

Steam iron and ironing board. These are essential for fabric preparation and for use throughout project construction.

Pins and mini sewing clips. You'll need some good-quality pins for holding fabric pieces together. When the fabric layers are thick, a set of mini sewing clips will be really useful. They're also perfect for use with laminated cotton to avoid leaving puncture marks. ④

Sewing thread. All-purpose polyester or cotton sewing-machine thread will work well; choose good-quality thread. It's a bit more expensive but well worth the price for quality, strength, and durability. ⑤

Sewing machine. All of these projects are sewn by machine. You don't need an expensive machine; a basic model will suffice. It must be capable of consistent straight stitches and have variable stitch length and a reverse (backstitching) function.

Air-soluble fabric marker or chalk. You can mark on fabric with tailor's chalk or an air-soluble fabric marker. The ink from the marker disappears after a little while, leaving no trace; always test it on a spare scrap of fabric. ⑥

Seam ripper. Seam rippers are the perfect tool for removing unwanted stitches quickly and neatly. They're also useful for cutting little slits into fabric when attaching magnetic snaps or starting the cutting lines for a zippered pocket. ⑦

Snap-attachment pliers. With interchangeable attachments, snap pliers are used for punching small holes through fabric layers and for squeezing metal snap parts together. Packs of snaps usually come with a disposable tool, but this can be difficult to use. I find the pliers indispensable for making the process really quick and easy. ⑧

Double-sided tape. Although not essential, double-sided tape can be very useful for holding pieces of Velcro or zipper edges in place temporarily while they are sewn to fabric pieces. I find this basting method much easier than using pins.

Fabric glue, cording, and flat-edged tool. A strong, permanent fabric glue is required for installing metal purse frames. Twisted paper cord or piping cord is also useful for creating a really good bond between the frame and the fabric edges. An old dinner knife, a pair of scissors, or a flat-head screwdriver can be used for pushing the fabric and cord into the purse frame channels. ⑨

Fabric Preparation

It's really important to prepare fabrics before cutting and sewing. Not only does preparation allow you to cut and sew the pieces accurately, it also enables you to achieve a professional finish.

BEFORE YOU BEGIN A PROJECT

If you'd like your bags to be machine washable, you'll need to prewash all the fabrics to get any shrinkage out of the way before you begin construction. Follow the manufacturer's instructions for washing and drying. If you intend for your bag to be spot-cleaned, then prewashing isn't necessary.

Whether they are prewashed or not, fabrics require a really good pressing with steam before use. This provides a crisp, flat surface to work with. It's impossible to remove any stubborn creases after completing a project, so use extra sprays of water and plenty of steam power as you press.

PRESSING DURING CONSTRUCTION

Within each project are instructions to press at particular steps; this is crucial for professional construction and a clean finish with crisp folds, neat pleats, and flat seam allowances. Failing to press a particular part when directed can lead to lopsided, poorly assembled pieces with bulky edges, so pressing is essential for neatness and accuracy throughout the project.

Interfacing

Many interfacings sold in the United States, especially Pellon products, are 20" wide, and that's reflected in the materials list for each project. If you're using Vilene products, which are 35½" wide, you'll need less yardage; be sure to recalculate the amount before purchasing your interfacing.

WHAT IS INTERFACING?

Interfacing is woven or nonwoven material hidden between the outer and lining layers of projects to add strength, stability, shape, and body. It can be fusible or sew-in and is an essential part of bag making.

Interfacing is available in different weights (thicknesses) and textures. As a rule of thumb for fusible interfacing, it's best to use one slightly lighter in weight than your fabric; this helps to avoid creases that might appear in the fabric. With the sew-in types, you can use heavier weights if required. Fusible interfacing, fusible fleece, and sew-in interfacing can be used together, allowing you to make a really strong bag that will stand up on its own and survive the test of time.

To assist you in choosing the right interfacings for the projects, I've noted the ones I used in the materials lists. I like to use Pellon or Vilene products as they are high in quality, and the fusible ones adhere to fabrics extremely well. They have loads of tiny little dots of glue, rather than a solid layer of glue, which helps the product adhere smoothly to the fabric without creasing and bubbling.

FUSIBLE VS. SEW-IN INTERFACING

Fusible interfacing makes a piece of fabric stiffer and hard wearing, and fusible fleece adds a layer of light padding. Depending on the type of interfacing you use, it can still leave the fabric with a nice, soft drape. Fusible interfacing has a shiny or bumpy side where fabric glue has been applied. This side is adhered permanently to the wrong side of the fabric with heat from an iron. Because it's fusible, you can cut it smaller than the fabric piece, trimming away the interfacing seam allowances to avoid bulk within the seams.

Sew-in interfacing gives a project stability with very slight padding and stops a bag from being floppy. It's usually cut to the same size as the fabric piece and basted to the fabric within the seam allowance; it's permanently sewn into the seams during construction.

APPLYING FUSIBLE INTERFACING

Fusible interfacings have instructions printed on a paper or plastic wrapper or along the fabric edges, giving the correct iron heat setting and pressing time and an indication whether a damp pressing cloth or steam is required for proper adhesion. If you've never used a particular interfacing before, it's best to experiment with some fabric scraps.

Press the fabric first, and then lay it flat on the ironing board, wrong side up. Lay the interfacing piece on top, glue side down, matching the edges, centering the interfacing, or positioning it as instructed in the project. Preheat the iron to the correct heat setting and then, starting from the center and working toward the edges, begin pressing one section at a time. Use an up-and-down motion, rather than a gliding motion. When you move to a different section, allow the iron to overlap the parts already fused, preventing air bubbles and gaps. Once the whole piece is fused, I like to carefully turn the piece right side up and glide the iron over its entirety to ensure a smooth finish. When finished, pick up the fabric very carefully to avoid creasing it and lay it on a flat surface. Leave it to cool completely, at least 30 minutes, before using; the cooling process is when the bond becomes permanent. Once the interfaced fabric is ready to use, treat the piece as one layer.

CHOOSING AN INTERFACING

Deciding which interfacing is best for a particular project can be confusing, as there are so many varieties, each with its own use. I've listed here the ones I've used in the projects. All of these work really well with medium-weight cottons.

Pellon ES114 Easy-Shaper/Vilene F220. Lightweight fusible nonwoven interfacing that is easy to adhere to the fabric and has a soft hand, allowing the fabric to retain a nice drape.

Pellon SF101 Shape-Flex/Vilene G700. Medium-weight fusible woven cotton interfacing with superior quality and an exceptionally soft hand, allowing the fabric to retain its drape while adding strength and support. Extremely easy to adhere to fabric, goes on beautifully. My favorite!

Pellon 930 Sew-In/Vilene M12. Medium-weight, sew-in interfacing. Can be used on its own or in conjunction with fusible interfacing if you need a durable, substantial bag. This interfacing is not too thick and is very soft and flexible.

Pellon 987F Fusible Fleece/Vilene H630. Low-loft, fusible fleece. Can be used on its own or with woven or nonwoven fusible interfacing. Once you've adhered interfacing to your fabric, the fleece can be fused on top of the interfacing to give the fabric a smooth and flexible feel, with the added benefit of soft padding from the fleece. It's perfect for projects that require a little padded protection. I also use small squares of fusible fleece for reinforcement when attaching magnetic snap closures.

Sewing Terms

This section provides explanations of the sewing terms I use throughout the projects.

Seam allowance. This is the space between the fabric edge and the stitches in a seam. To achieve an even seam allowance, place the edge of the fabric at the relevant marking on the sewing-machine needle plate and watch the fabric edge, not the needle, as you sew to keep the seam allowance even. When you can't see the needle plate, use edges or markings on the presser foot as a guide.

Baste. Sew long, evenly spaced straight stitches to hold fabric layers in place temporarily. You can sew a running stitch by hand, but it's much quicker and easier to use the longest stitch length on your sewing machine. Machine-baste within the project seam allowance so that you don't have to remove the stitches.

Press. Using a steam iron, press sections as indicated in the project instructions to form neat folds and pleats, to flatten a seam allowance, or to eliminate excessive creasing.

Topstitching provides a decorative touch.

Press seam allowances open or toward one side. Use a steam iron to flatten the seam allowances, either by opening up the two edges and pressing them flat or by folding the two edges to the same side and pressing. It's really important to follow these steps to avoid bulk at the seams and to strengthen joining seams. ❶

Topstitch. Topstitching is both functional and decorative. It's functional in that it joins fabric layers and strengthens seams. It's decorative because the stitching will be seen. Adjust the stitch length when topstitching to suit the thickness of the fabric layers you're sewing; a longer stitch setting is necessary to maintain actual stitch length when many layers are being fed through the machine. A contrasting thread color can be used so that the stitches stand out, which is quite effective in adding interest to the design.

Backstitch. To secure stitching at the beginning and end of the seam, use the sewing machine's reverse function to sew a few stitches backward along the seamline, securing the forward stitches.

Notch or clip curved edges. Curved fabric edges will bunch or pull when turned right side out unless you cut into the seam allowances to release them or remove some fabric to reduce their bulk. For outward (convex) curves, notch the curved edge by clipping small, evenly spaced triangles from the seam allowances. ❷

For inward (concave) curves, simply clip straight into the seam allowances at regular intervals or cut out narrow triangles. In both cases, avoid cutting through the line of stitching. ❸

Trim the corners. Cut diagonally across each stitched corner to remove the triangular point, being careful not to clip the stitching. This will reduce bulk at the corners when the layers are turned right side out. ❹

❶

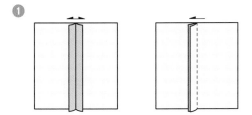

❷

❸

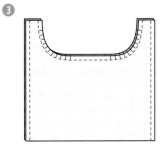

❹

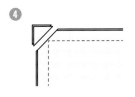

Bag-Making Techniques

Once you've gotten the hang of some basic techniques, bag making is quite an easy process. Many techniques are used often, so I've put together some mini tutorials for you to refer to as required.

PIN PLACEMENT

Placing pins at a 90° angle to the fabric edges holds the fabric layers together with less shifting. You can stitch with the pins in place to avoid basting; just remove each pin as it approaches the presser foot and needle.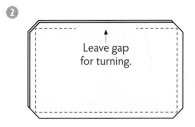

STITCH LENGTHS

Straight stitching is used throughout these projects. The stitch-length setting should be approximately 2.5 mm (10 stitches per inch) in most cases, increasing to 3 to 3.5 mm (7 to 9 stitches per inch) for thicker layers to allow the needle and bobbin threads to lock together properly. When sew-in interfacing is used, increase the stitch length a little to compensate for the extra bulk, and increase the stitch length for the portion of a seam that crosses a handle, tab, or flap end. Also use a longer stitch for topstitching, as the layers will be thicker and the longer stitches look more appealing. When machine basting, use the longest stitch length available.

POCKETS

Pockets are optional in these projects. You can choose to leave them out or add extra pockets to suit your needs.

Lined Patch Pocket

1 | Place the main pocket and pocket lining pieces right sides together. Stitch all the sides, using a ⅜" seam allowance, leaving a gap at the center of the top edge for turning. Trim the corners diagonally.

2 | Turn the pocket right side out, using a point turner or other tool to work the corners into place, and press. Fold the edges to the wrong side along the seamline across the gap; press and pin the opening closed. Topstitch ⅛" from the top edge of the pocket, closing the gap.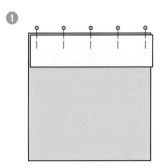

Topstitch top edge,
closing the gap as you stitch.

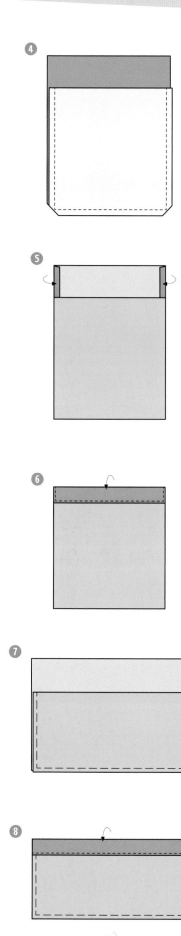

Bordered Patch Pocket

1 | Place the main pocket and pocket lining pieces right sides together, matching the bottom and side edges. Stitch both sides and the bottom edge with a ⅜" seam allowance. Trim the bottom corners diagonally. **4**

2 | Turn the pocket right side out, using a point turner or other tool to work the corners into place. Press the pocket, pressing the remaining raw edges to the wrong side along the side seamlines. **5**

3 | Fold the top edge of the lining down to meet the top edge of the main pocket and press. Fold the lining again, along the line where the two pieces meet, so that the lining overlaps the main pocket. Press again and pin. Topstitch ⅛" from the sides and lower edge of the lining overlap. **6**

Bordered Sew-In Pocket

1 | Place the main pocket and lining pieces with wrong sides together, aligning the bottom and side edges. Pin. Baste the bottom and side edges of the pocket ¼" from the raw edges. **7**

2 | Fold the top edge of the lining down to meet the top edge of the main pocket and press. Fold the lining again, along the line where the two pieces meet, so that the lining overlaps the main pocket. Press again and pin. Topstitch ⅛" from the lower edge of the lining overlap. The sides and bottom will be finished later. **8**

BOXED BAG BASE

A flat base is easily created by boxing the bottom corners of the outer bag and lining before they are sewn together.

1 | Flatten the outer bag, wrong side out, aligning the side seam with the bottom seam at one bottom corner. Pin. Draw a line across each corner, perpendicular to the seam, at the point where the width across the corner matches the depth indicated in the project instructions. For example: if a bag should be 3" deep, measure 1½" from the seamline intersection at the bottom corner to draw a line 3" long.

LINE THEM UP

For perfect results when boxing a bag, pin through the side and bottom seamlines to align the seams exactly.

2 | Stitch on the marked line, backstitching at each end of the seam. Trim the excess fabric from the corner, leaving ⅜" seam allowances. **9**

3 | Repeat steps 1 and 2 to box the remaining bag corner and both lining corners, creating a flat bottom for the bag.

FABRIC HANDLES

There's a good selection of ready-made handles on the market, but I like to make fabric handles, as it saves money—and they look fab, too! I coordinate the handles or shoulder straps with the bag by using some of the main bag fabrics. Fabric handles can be stitched straight into the seams during construction, or you can add a professional touch by using metal hardware, such as D-rings, rectangular rings, adjustable slides, and swivel hooks.

Open-Ended Handle

This method is also used for making D-ring/rectangular-ring tabs.

1 | Fold the fabric in half lengthwise, wrong side together, and press. Open the fold and press the long edges to the wrong side so they meet at the center crease line.

2 | Refold along the center crease, enclosing the raw edges and aligning the folded edges on one side. Press and pin.

3 | Topstitch ⅛" from both long edges. **10**

Open-Ended Handle with Contrast Lining

1 | Press the long edges of a handle piece to the wrong side so the edges meet at the center, enclosing the applied interfacing. Repeat with a handle lining piece.

2 | Place the handle and lining pieces wrong sides together, enclosing the long raw edges. Align the edges and pin the layers together.

3 | Topstitch ⅛" from both long edges. **11**

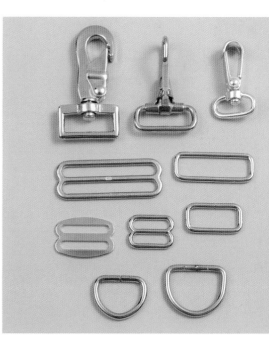

Selection of metal hardware used for some of the project handles

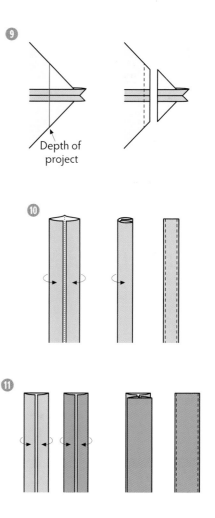

Closed-End Handle

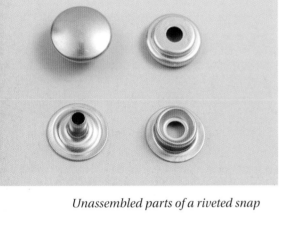

1 | Fold the fabric in half lengthwise, wrong side together, and press. Open the fold and press ½" to the wrong side on each short end.

2 | Fold the long edges to the wrong side so the edges meet at the center crease and press.

3 | Refold along the center crease, enclosing the raw edges and aligning the folded edges. Press and pin.

4 | Topstitch ⅛" from all four edges. ⑫

BAG CLOSURES

I've used different closure options throughout the book, but you don't have to stick to the one suggested for the project you're making. If you prefer to use magnetic snaps rather than riveted snaps, you'll need to attach them to the correct pattern piece during construction rather than at the end. You can also use sew-on Velcro if you prefer.

Riveted Snaps

Riveted snaps are attached when project construction is finished. Use them at the top edges of bag openings as a main closure, and for tab or flap closures. For installation, you'll need a ruler and an air-soluble fabric marker or a pencil.

1 | Measure and mark the location for the front of the snap as directed in the project instructions or as desired. Take your time to check the position, making sure it is centered.

2 | Punch a hole through the fabric layers at the marked position, using pliers or the disposable tool that came with the snaps.

3 | Fold the project so the front and back are aligned. Mark a dot straight through the snap hole, onto the corresponding back part of the project, to pinpoint the exact position of the hole required for the back half of the snap. Punch the hole.

Unassembled parts of a riveted snap

A riveted snap used to close the upper edge of a bag

4 | Place the front half of the snap into the pliers or disposable tool, following the manufacturer's instructions. Position the tool around the hole you made in the front of the project and squeeze gently to bring the parts of the snap together. Once you're sure the parts are correctly aligned, squeeze the pliers tightly to seat the snap firmly. Repeat this step to attach the back half of the snap through the other hole.

Magnetic Snaps

Standard magnetic snaps are attached to projects during construction. They offer a hidden fastener that's easy to open and close. For installation, you'll need a ruler, an air-soluble fabric marker or pencil, and a seam ripper or small, sharp scissors.

1 | Transfer the snap position from the project pattern to the right side of the corresponding fabric piece. Alternatively, find the centerline of the project, use a ruler to measure how far from the top edge you want the snap to be, and mark the center point of the snap location. Adhere a 1" square of fusible fleece to the wrong side of the fabric, centering the fleece on the snap location. Place the snap's back plate on the right side of the fabric, centering it on the snap location, and mark through the two slit openings.

2 | Cut tiny slits at the marked positions, through all of the layers, using a seam ripper or small, sharp scissors. Insert the snap prongs through the slits from the right side.

3 | Place the back plate over the prongs on the fabric wrong side. Hold it firmly in place while you fold the prongs outward.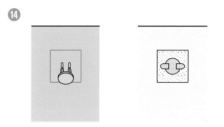

4 | Repeat steps 1–3 to attach the other half of the snap to the corresponding fabric piece, or as indicated in the project instructions.

Use the snap back plate to mark slit positions.

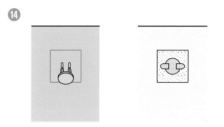

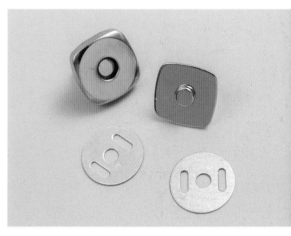

Unassembled magnetic-snap parts

A magnetic snap on a tab closure

A covered button adds a decorative feature.

Covered Buttons

Covered buttons are a great way to add a coordinating decorative feature to a project. They're really easy to make and only require a small scrap of fabric. Button forms are available in plastic or metal, and can be purchased in kits that may include a tool for assembly.

1 | Cut out the circular template from the button-kit packaging for the size of button you are covering.

> ### FEATURING FABRIC
>
> You can make your own pattern for a covered button. Use vellum or transparent paper, and the pattern becomes a guide for fussy cutting, allowing you to feature an area of the fabric on the button.
>
> Trace the button form onto transparent paper. Draw a second circle around the first, ½" larger for a 1"-diameter button or ¾" larger for a 1½"-diameter button. The inner circle is a guide to the fabric area that will be seen on the finished button. Cut out the template along the larger circle.

2 | Use the template to cut a circle of fabric for the button. If your fabric is thin, or you want to achieve a more padded appearance, you can add a circle of interfacing to the fabric wrong side.

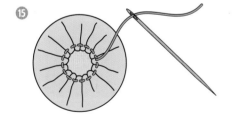

3 | Follow the manufacturer's instructions for wrapping the button form with your fabric. If your fabric is thick or stiff, you may find it helpful to run a line of gathering stitches around the edge of the fabric. After centering the button form on the fabric wrong side, pull the thread to tighten the gathering stitches, pulling the fabric into place around the button form. **⑮**

4 | Position the back plate of the button and push it down firmly to lock it into place. Pushing the back plate into position also tightens the fabric around the button form.

PROJECTS

FUNKY HANDBAG

Stitch a fun handbag in bright, retro-style fabrics, just perfect for a special event or evening out. Try teaming polka dots with a coordinating floral fabric to achieve this funky look.

SKILL LEVEL: Beginner

FINISHED BAG SIZE: approximately 13½" x 10½"

TECHNIQUES:

- Lined Patch Pocket (page 13)
- Open-Ended Handle (page 15)
- Riveted Snaps (page 16)

MATERIALS

Yardage is based on 42"-wide fabric and 20"-wide interfacing.

⅜ yard of fabric A for outer bag

⅝ yard of fabric B for top bands, handles, and pocket

⅜ yard of fabric C for lining

1 yard of fusible woven interfacing (Pellon SF101)*

One ⅝" riveted snap

*If you use a 35½"-wide interfacing such as Vilene G700, purchase ⅝ yard.

CUTTING

See "Good to Know" on page 22 for information on seam allowances and pattern pieces.

From fabric A, cut:
2 main-bag pieces, for outer bag

From fabric B, cut:
4 rectangles, 3" x 11¼", for top bands
2 strips, 5" x 21", for handles
2 rectangles, 7" x 9", for pocket

From fabric C, cut:
2 main-bag pieces, for lining

From the fusible interfacing, cut:
4 main-bag pieces, for outer bag and lining
4 rectangles, 3" x 11¼", for top bands
2 strips, 2½" x 21", for handles
1 rectangle, 7" x 9", for pocket

"Funky Handbag," made with fabric from the Nördika Collection by Jeni Baker for Art Gallery Fabrics

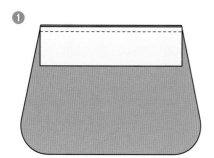

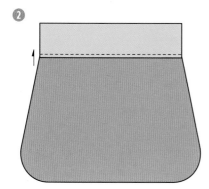

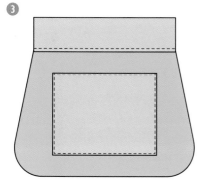

Topstitch.

PREPARATION

Fuse the interfacing pieces to the wrong side of the corresponding fabric pieces. Center the handle interfacing pieces on the fabric handles and fuse.

TOP BANDS

1 | With right sides together, stitch the bottom edge of a top band to the top edge of an outer bag. Repeat to join a second top band to the remaining outer bag. **①**

2 | Press the seam allowances toward the top bands and topstitch ¼" from the seam. **②**

3 | Repeat steps 1 and 2 to join and topstitch the remaining top bands to the lining pieces.

POCKET

1 | Make the pocket, referring to "Lined Patch Pocket."

2 | With both pieces right side up, center the pocket on one lining piece and pin. Topstitch ⅛" from the sides and bottom edge of the pocket. **③**

OUTER BAG AND LINING

1 | Place the outer-bag units right sides together, matching the band seams and aligning all the edges. Pin. Stitch the sides and bottom edge.

2 | Notch the curved edges. Clip the seam allowances above and below the band seams, being careful not to cut through the stitches. Press the seam allowances open. ❹

3 | Turn the outer bag right side out, smoothing the edges into place. Press lightly, using a pressing cloth.

4 | Repeat steps 1 and 2 to sew the lining units together, but leave a 5" gap at the center bottom for turning. Leave the lining wrong side out.

HANDLES

1 | Make two handles, referring to "Open-Ended Handles."

2 | Pin the ends of one handle to the front of the outer bag, matching the raw edges and positioning the handle ends 1½" from the bag's side seams. Be sure the handle isn't twisted, and baste ¼" from the raw edges. Pin and baste the ends of the other handle to the back of the outer bag in the same way. ❺

BAG ASSEMBLY

1 | Insert the outer bag into the lining, right sides together, matching the side seams and aligning the top edges; pin. Be sure the handles are tucked out of the way between the layers. As you align the side seams, be sure the seam allowances remain open to reduce bulk when the layers are sewn together.

2 | Stitch around the top edge. ❻

3 | Turn the bag and lining right side out through the gap in the lining seam. Press both sections lightly, using a pressing cloth. Press the seam allowances to the wrong side along the lining gap and pin. Stitch the gap closed by hand, or machine stitch very close to the pressed edges.

4 | Tuck the lining inside the outer bag and smooth into place. Press the top edges so that the seam sits neatly at the top. Topstitch ¼" from the top edge of the bag. ❼

5 | Attach the snap parts, centering them on the front and back top bands, referring to "Riveted Snaps."

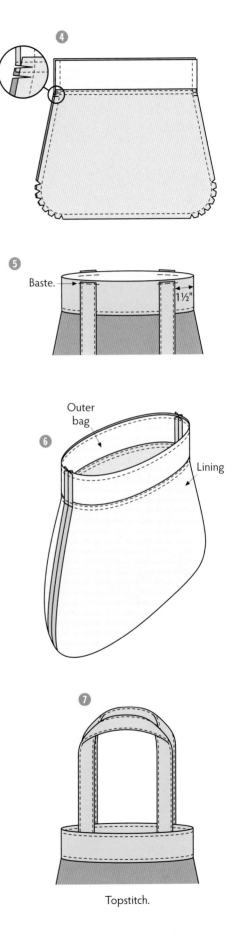

Baste.

1½"

Outer bag

Lining

Topstitch.

Funky Handbag
Cut 2 on fold from fabric A for outer bag.
Cut 2 on fold from fabric C for lining.
Cut 4 on fold from fusible interfacing.

Place on fold.

⅜" seam allowance

LARGE MARKET BAG

Go shopping in style with a large market bag. The tote boasts roomy pockets that can be sewn to either the exterior or the interior of the bag to suit your needs. Try mixing a cool, contemporary print with a coordinating deep color to add spice.

SKILL LEVEL: Confident Beginner

FINISHED BAG SIZE: approximately 19¼" x 16½"

TECHNIQUES:

- Bordered Sew-In Pocket (page 14)
- Open-Ended Handle (page 15)
- Riveted Snaps (page 16)

MATERIALS

Yardage is based on 42"-wide fabric and 20"-wide interfacing.

½ yard of fabric A for outer bag

⅝ yard of fabric B for pockets and handles

⅝ yard of fabric C for pocket lining and top bands

⅝ yard of fabric D for lining and top-band lining

2⅛ yards of fusible woven interfacing (Pellon SF101)*

⅞ yard of sew-in interfacing (Pellon 930)*

One ⅝" riveted snap

*If you use 35½"-wide interfacing, purchase 1⅜ yards of the fusible woven interfacing (Vilene G700) and ⅝ yard of the sew-in (Vilene M12).

CUTTING

From fabric A, cut:
2 rectangles, 15" x 20", for outer bag

From fabric B, cut:
2 rectangles, 10" x 20", for pockets
2 strips, 6" x 21", for handles

From fabric C, cut:
2 rectangles, 14" x 20", for pocket lining
2 rectangles, 3" x 16", for top bands

From fabric D, cut:
2 rectangles, 15" x 20", for lining
2 rectangles, 3" x 16", for top-band lining

From the fusible interfacing, cut:
2 rectangles, 15" x 20", for outer bag
2 rectangles, 10" x 20", for pockets
4 rectangles, 3" x 16", for top bands
2 strips, 3" x 21", for handles

From the sew-in interfacing, cut:
2 rectangles, 15" x 20", for outer-bag lining

"Large Market Bag," made with fabric from the Winter's Lane collection by Kate & Birdie Paper Co. for Moda Fabrics

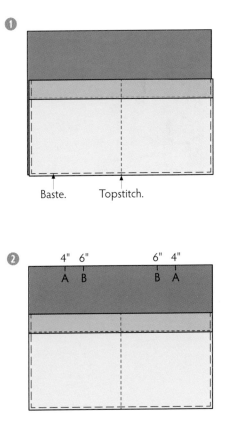

PREPARATION

1 | Fuse the interfacing pieces to the wrong side of the corresponding fabric pieces. Center the handle interfacing pieces on the fabric handles and fuse.

2 | Pin a sew-in interfacing rectangle to the wrong side of each lining rectangle. Baste ¼" from the edges.

POCKETS

1 | Make two pockets, referring to "Bordered Sew-In Pocket."

2 | With right sides up, position and pin one of the pockets on an outer-bag piece, aligning the bottom and side edges. Mark a vertical line along the center of the pocket to divide it into two equal pockets. Topstitch on the line. Baste the sides and bottom edge of the pocket to the bag ¼" from the edge. ❶

3 | Repeat step 2 to attach the other pocket to the remaining outer bag.

PLEATS

1 | With one of the outer-bag pieces right side up, measure and mark the A and B positions along the top long edge, 4" and 6" from each side seam. ❷

❶ Baste.   Topstitch.

❷ 4" 6"   6" 4"
    A B   B A

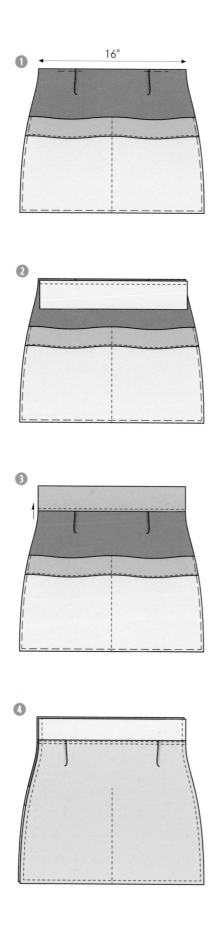

2 | Fold the fabric, wrong sides together, at one point A. Bring A to meet the nearest point B and pin. Repeat at the other A and B positions. The top edge of the outer bag should now measure 16"; adjust the pleats if required. Baste the pleats ¼" from the edge. ❶

3 | Repeat steps 1 and 2 to add pleats to the second outer bag and both lining pieces.

TOP BANDS

1 | With right sides together, stitch the bottom edge of a top band to the pleated edge of an outer bag. Repeat to join the second top band to the remaining outer bag. ❷

2 | Press the seam allowances toward the top bands and topstitch ¼" from the seam. ❸

3 | Repeat steps 1 and 2 to assemble and topstitch the lining and top-band lining.

BAG AND LINING

1 | Place the outer-bag units right sides together. Align and pin the top-band seams and the contrasting bands of the pockets, and then the full side and bottom edges. Stitch the sides and bottom. ❹

ON THE INCREASE

You may need to increase the stitch length as you stitch through the pocket sections, because more layers make the project thicker there.

2 | Trim the corners diagonally and clip into the seam allowances above and below the top-band seams, taking care not to clip the stitching. Press the seam allowances open. Turn the bag right side out, using a point turner or other tool to smooth the corners into place.

3 | Repeat steps 1 and 2 to sew the lining units together, leaving an 8" gap at the center bottom for turning. Leave the lining wrong side out.

HANDLES

1 | Make two handles, referring to "Open-Ended Handle."

2 | Pin the ends of one handle to the front outer bag, matching the raw edges and positioning the handle ends 3" from the bag's side seams. Be sure that the handle isn't twisted and baste ¼" from the raw edges. Pin and baste the other handle ends to the back outer bag in the same way. ⑤

BAG ASSEMBLY

1 | Insert the outer bag into the lining, right sides together, matching the side seams and aligning the top edges; pin. Be sure the handles are tucked out of the way between the layers. Stitch the top edge. ⑥

2 | Turn the bag and lining right side out through the gap in the lining seam. Press both sections lightly, using a pressing cloth.

3 | Press the seam allowances to the wrong side along the gap in the lining. Stitch the gap closed, either by hand or with machine stitches placed close to the pressed edges.

4 | Tuck the lining inside the outer bag and smooth into place. Press the top edge so that the seam sits neatly at the top, pressing the handles away from the bag. Topstitch ¼" from the edge around the opening of the bag. ⑦

5 | Attach the snap parts, centering them on the front and back top bands. Refer to "Riveted Snaps."

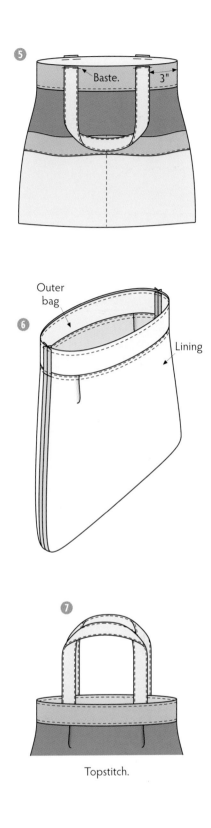

Baste. 3"

Outer bag

Lining

Topstitch.

UPTOWN SHOPPER

Sew a luxurious tote bag for an uptown shopping trip. This project is perfect for using complementary medium-weight cottons. Choose a vibrant print for the main fabric, teaming it with coordinating solids to achieve a rich, dramatic look.

SKILL LEVEL: Confident Beginner

FINISHED BAG SIZE: approximately 16¼" x 15¼" x 4"

TECHNIQUES:
- Bordered Patch Pocket (page 14)
- Boxed Bag Base (page 14)
- Open-Ended Handle with Contrast Lining (page 15)

MATERIALS

Yardage is based on 42"-wide fabric and 20"-wide interfacing.

¾ yard of fabric A for outer bag, pocket, handles, and tab

⅝ yard of fabric B for upper bag, pocket, and handles

⅝ yard of fabric C for lining

2⅜ yards of fusible woven interfacing (Pellon SF101)*

1¼ yards of sew-in interfacing (Pellon 930)*

3¾" x 11½" piece of plastic canvas for bag bottom

2" length of 1½"-wide Velcro

*If you use 35½"-wide interfacing, purchase 1½ yards of the fusible woven interfacing (Vilene G700) and ¾ yard of the sew-in (Vilene M12).

CUTTING

From fabric A, cut:
2 rectangles, 12⅜" x 17", for outer bag
1 square, 10" x 10", for pocket
2 strips, 3" x 21", for handles
2 rectangles, 4" x 5", for tab

From fabric B, cut:
2 rectangles, 6⅜" x 17", for upper bag
1 rectangle, 10" x 12", for pocket lining
2 strips, 3½" x 21", for handle lining

From fabric C, cut:
2 rectangles, 17" x 18", for lining

From the fusible interfacing, cut:
2 rectangles, 12⅜" x 17", for outer bag
2 rectangles, 6⅜" x 17", for upper bag
2 rectangles, 17" x 18", for lining
1 square, 10" x 10", for pocket
2 strips, 1¾" x 21", for handle lining
2 rectangles, 4" x 5", for tab

Continued on page 32

"Uptown Shopper," made with fabric from the Heritage collection by Beth Logan for Robert Kaufman Fabrics

A Velcro fastener is used for the tab closure.

Continued from page 30

From the sew-in interfacing, cut:

2 rectangles, 17" x 18", for pieced outer bag

2 strips, 1½" x 21", for handles

1 rectangle, 4" x 5", for tab

GOOD TO KNOW

- All seam allowances are included in the cutting instructions.
- Seam allowances are ⅜" throughout, unless stated otherwise.

PREPARATION

Fuse the interfacing pieces to the wrong side of the corresponding fabric pieces. Center the handle interfacing on the handle lining pieces and fuse.

OUTER BAG

1 | With right sides together, sew the bottom edge of an upper bag to the top edge of an outer-bag piece. Make two.

2 | Press the seam allowances toward the upper bag and topstitch ¼" from the seams. These are the outer-bag units.

3 | Pin the corresponding sew-in interfacing to the wrong sides of the outer-bag units and baste ¼" from the edges.

4 | Choose one outer bag as the front of the bag. Center one half of the Velcro fastener on the right side of the bag front, 1" below the top edge of the bag. Pin in place and topstitch ⅛" from all four edges of the fastener to secure it. ❶

STICK TO IT

Try using double-sided tape to hold the Velcro fastener in place instead of pins.

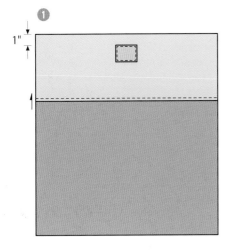

POCKET

1 │ Make the pocket, referring to "Bordered Patch Pocket."

2 │ With both pieces right side up, center the pocket on one lining piece. Pin in place. Stitch ⅛" from the sides and bottom edge of the pocket.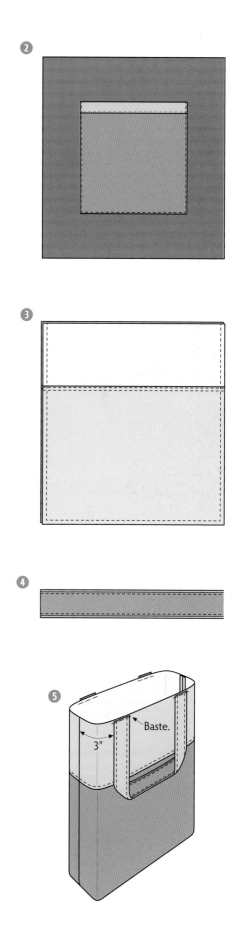

BAG AND LINING

1 │ Place the outer-bag units right sides together, matching the horizontal seams and aligning all the edges; pin. Stitch the sides and lower edge.

2 │ Press the seam allowances open. Leave the outer bag wrong side out. ❸

3 │ Repeat steps 1 and 2 to sew the lining pieces together, but leave a 6" gap at the center bottom for turning. Leave the lining wrong side out.

4 │ Box the corners of the outer bag and lining to create a depth of 4", referring to "Boxed Bag Base." Turn the outer bag right side out; leave the lining wrong side out.

HANDLES

1 │ Center the corresponding sew-in interfacing pieces on the wrong sides of the handle pieces (the ones without fusible interfacing).

2 │ Make two handles, referring to "Open-Ended Handle with Contrast Lining." The handles cut from fabric A are narrower than those cut from fabric B. Center a prepared A handle piece on each B handle piece, rather than aligning the long edges of the handles, to create a contrasting border on the right side of the finished handle. Topstitch ⅛" from the pressed folds of the fabric A handles to join the pieces. ❹

3 │ With right sides together, pin the ends of one handle to the outer-bag front, matching the raw edges and positioning the handle ends 3" from the bag's side seams. Be sure that the handle isn't twisted and baste ¼" from the raw edges. Pin and baste the other handle to the outer bag back in the same way. ❺

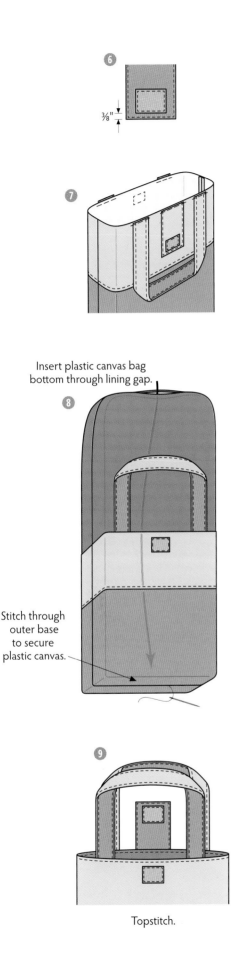

3/8"

Insert plastic canvas bag bottom through lining gap.

Stitch through outer base to secure plastic canvas.

Topstitch.

TAB

1 | Place the tab pieces right sides together and layer the sew-in interfacing piece on the bottom. Pin the layers together. Stitch three sides, leaving one short edge open. Trim the bottom corners diagonally to reduce bulk.

2 | Turn the tab right side out, using a point turner to smooth the corners into place, and press. Topstitch ⅛" from the stitched edges, leaving the short edge open.

3 | Choose which side of the tab will be the lining side and center the other half of the Velcro fastener ⅜" from the stitched short edge. Pin or tape in place. Stitch ⅛" from all four edges of the fastener to secure. ❻

4 | With right sides together, center the tab closure on the back outer bag, matching the raw edges. Baste ¼" from the raw edges. ❼

BAG ASSEMBLY

1 | Insert the outer bag into the lining with right sides together, matching the side seams and aligning the top edges, and pin. Be sure the handles and the tab are tucked out of the way between the layers. Stitch the top edge.

2 | Turn the outer bag and lining right side out through the opening in the lining seam. Press both sections lightly, using a pressing cloth.

3 | Insert the plastic canvas bag bottom through the gap in the lining and position it at the base of the outer bag. Hand sew a few securing stitches through the bag base and plastic canvas, hiding the stitches in the bag's bottom seam, to keep the plastic canvas in place. ❽

4 | Press the seam allowances to the wrong side along the gap in the lining seam. Stitch the gap closed, either by hand or with machine stitches placed close to the pressed edges.

5 | Tuck the lining inside the outer bag and smooth it into place. Press the top edge of the bag so that the seam sits neatly at the top, pressing the handles and tab away from the bag. Topstitch ¼" from the upper edge. ❾

PLEATED CLUTCH

Stitch a sophisticated clutch for a special event. You won't have to search for the perfect purse to match your outfit; simply choose medium-weight fabrics to match perfectly. A fabric-covered button adds a decorative touch.

SKILL LEVEL: Confident Beginner

FINISHED PURSE SIZE: approximately 11¾" x 9½"

TECHNIQUES:

- Lined Patch Pocket (page 13)
- Covered Buttons (page 18)

MATERIALS

Yardage is based on 42"-wide fabric, 20"-wide interfacing, and 45"-wide fusible fleece.

⅜ yard of fabric A for outer bag and top bands

¼ yard of fabric B for pocket

¼ yard of fabric C for flap

⅜ yard of fabric D for lining

⅞ yard of fusible nonwoven interfacing (Pellon ES114)*

⅜ yard of fusible fleece (Pellon 987F)*

2" length of 1½"-wide Velcro

1½"-diameter button form or button

Air-soluble fabric marker or chalk

*If you use 35½"-wide interfacing, purchase ½ yard of the fusible nonwoven interfacing (Vilene F220) and ⅜ yard of the fusible fleece (Vilene H630)

CUTTING

See "Good to Know" on page 37 for information on seam allowances and pattern pieces.

From fabric A, cut:
2 main-bag pieces, for outer bag
2 rectangles, 3⅛" x 10¼", for top bands

From fabric B, cut:
2 rectangles, 5½" x 8½", for pocket

From fabric C, cut:
1 flap piece

From fabric D, cut:
2 bag-lining pieces
2 rectangles, 3⅛" x 10¼", for top-band lining
1 flap piece, for lining

From the fusible interfacing, cut:
2 main-bag pieces
4 rectangles, 3⅛" x 10¼", for top bands
2 flap pieces
1 rectangle, 5½" x 8½", for pocket

From the fusible fleece, cut:
2 bag-lining pieces
1 flap piece

"Pleated Clutch," made with fabrics from the Juggling Summer collection by Brigitte Heitland for Zen Chic, for Moda Fabrics

A Velcro fastener is used for the closure.

PREPARATION

1 | Fuse the interfacing pieces to the wrong side of the corresponding fabric pieces.

2 | Center the corresponding fleece pieces on the wrong side of the lining pieces and fuse.

3 | Position the fleece flap on the wrong side of the fabric D flap, 1" below the straight top edge and centered from side to side, and fuse.

PLEATS

1 | Transfer the dots from the outer-bag pattern to the fabric. Connect the A dots and both pairs of B dots to make three vertical lines on each outer bag, using an air-soluble fabric marker or chalk. ❶

2 | Fold one outer bag, wrong sides together, along one B line. Bring the fold to meet the centerline (A); press and pin. Repeat with the second B line; the folds will meet at the centerline to form an inverted box pleat. Baste ¼" from the top and bottom edges to hold the folds in place. Make two. ❷

TOP BANDS

1 | With right sides together, stitch the bottom edge of a top band to the top of a prepared outer bag. Make two.

2 | Press the seam allowances toward the top bands and topstitch ¼" from the seam.

3 | Repeat steps 1 and 2 to join and topstitch the bag-lining and top-band lining pieces.

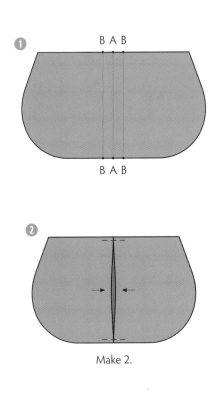

Make 2.

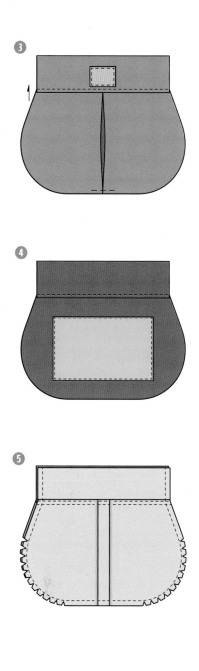

4 | Choose one outer-bag piece to be the purse front. Center one half of the Velcro fastener on the right side of the front's top-band panel and pin in place. Stitch ⅛" from the fastener edges to secure. ❸

STICK TO IT

You may find it easier to use double-sided tape, rather than pins, for holding the Velcro fastener in place.

POCKET

1 | Make the pocket, referring to "Lined Patch Pocket."

2 | With both pieces right side up, center the pocket on one lining piece and pin. Stitch ⅛" from the sides and bottom edge of the pocket. ❹

BAG AND LINING

1 | Place the outer-bag units right sides together, aligning the band seams and matching the pleats at the bottom edge, and pin.

2 | Stitch the sides and lower edge.

3 | Notch the curves and clip the seam allowances on both sides of the band seams, being careful not to cut the stitching. Press the seam allowances open. ❺

4 | Turn the bag right side out, smoothing all the edges and curves neatly. Lightly press, using a pressing cloth.

5 | Repeat steps 1–3 with the lining units, but leave a 6" gap at the center bottom for turning. Leave the lining wrong side out.

FLAP

1 | Place the two flap pieces right sides together and pin. Stitch the sides and bottom, leaving the straight top edge open. Notch the curved edges.

2 | Turn the flap right side out and press. Topstitch ⅛" from the side and bottom edges, leaving the straight top edge open.

3 | Center the remaining half of the Velcro fastener on the lining side of the flap, 1" from the curved edge. Pin in place (or use double-sided tape). Topstitch ⅛" from all four edges of the fastener to secure. ❻

4 | With right sides together, center the flap on the back outer bag, matching the raw edges, and pin. Baste ¼" from the edge. ❼

BAG ASSEMBLY

1 | Insert the outer bag into the lining, right sides together. Match the side seams, align the top edges, and pin. Be sure the flap is tucked out of the way between the layers. Stitch the top edge.

2 | Turn the outer bag and lining right side out through the gap in the lining seam. Press lightly, using a pressing cloth. Press the seam allowances to the wrong side along the opening in the lining and pin. Stitch the gap closed, either by hand or with machine stitches placed close to the pressed edges.

3 | Tuck the lining inside the outer bag and smooth everything into place. Press the top edges of the bag so that the seam sits neatly at the top, pressing the flap away from the seam. Topstitch ¼" from the upper edge of the bag. ❽

4 | Cover a button form with a scrap of the main fabric, referring to "Covered Buttons," or select a suitable ready-made button. Stitch the button securely to the right side of the flap, over the Velcro fastener.

Contrasting topstitching thread and a large fabric-covered button add exquisite finishing details.

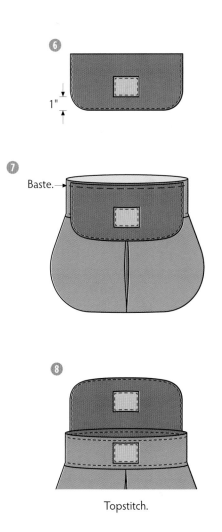

❻

1"

❼

Baste.

❽

Topstitch.

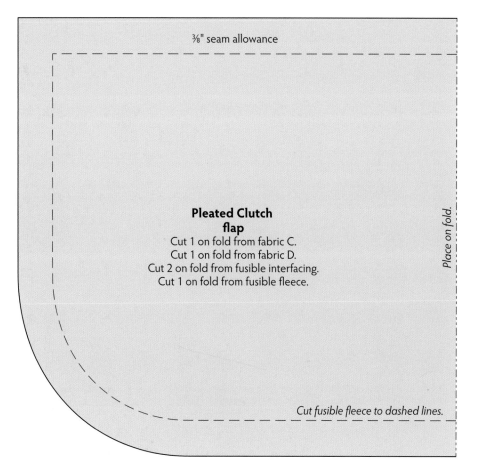

⅜" seam allowance

Place on fold.

**Pleated Clutch
flap**
Cut 1 on fold from fabric C.
Cut 1 on fold from fabric D.
Cut 2 on fold from fusible interfacing.
Cut 1 on fold from fusible fleece.

Cut fusible fleece to dashed lines.

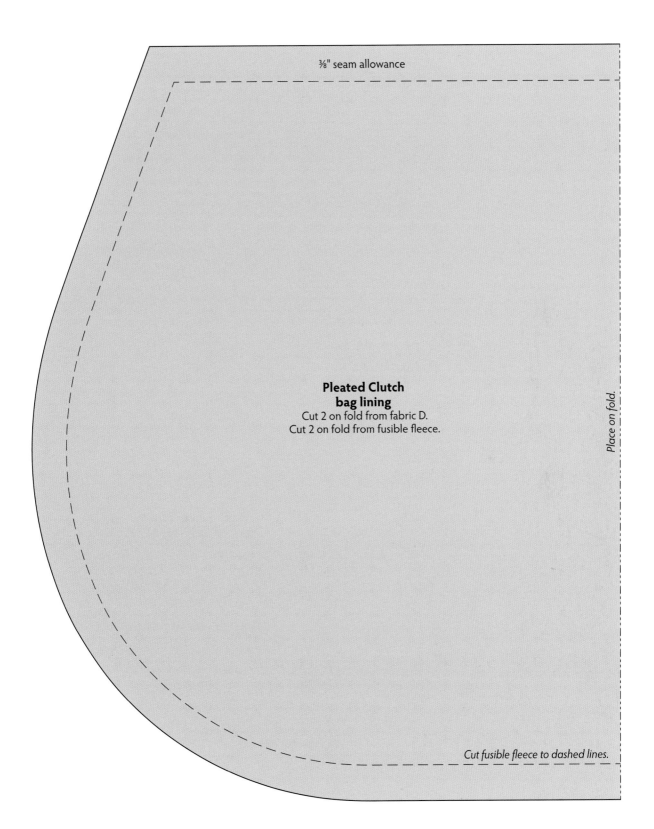

⅜" seam allowance

Pleated Clutch
bag lining
Cut 2 on fold from fabric D.
Cut 2 on fold from fusible fleece.

Place on fold.

Cut fusible fleece to dashed lines.

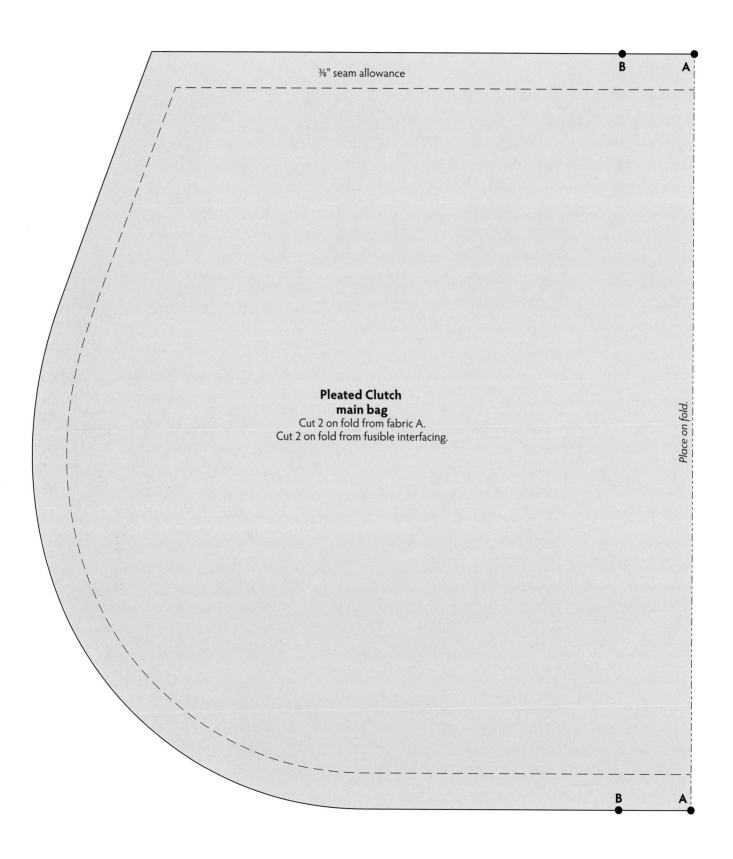

⅜" seam allowance

B   A

Pleated Clutch
main bag
Cut 2 on fold from fabric A.
Cut 2 on fold from fusible interfacing.

Place on fold.

B   A

HOBO HANDBAG

Accessorize your outfit perfectly with a cute little hobo-style handbag. Team a medium-weight cotton in a medium-scale print with a complementary solid fabric for a polished appearance.

SKILL LEVEL: Confident Beginner

FINISHED BAG SIZE: approximately 11¼" x 8¼" (at center front)

TECHNIQUES:

- Lined Patch Pocket (page 13)
- Open-Ended Handle (page 15)
- Magnetic Snaps (page 17)

MATERIALS

Yardage is based on 42"-wide fabric and 20"-wide interfacing.

½ yard of fabric A for outer bag, tab, and shoulder strap

⅜ yard of fabric B for lining

¼ yard of fabric C for center panel, tab, and pocket

1½ yards of fusible woven interfacing (Pellon SF101)*

Scraps of fusible fleece (Pellon 987F or Vilene H630)

One ½" magnetic snap (slim style if possible)

If you use 35½"-wide interfacing, purchase 1 yard of the fusible woven interfacing (Vilene G700).

CUTTING

See "Good to Know" on page 45 for information on seam allowances and pattern pieces.

From fabric A, cut:
2 main-bag pieces, for outer bag
1 tab piece
1 strip, 4¾" x 42", for shoulder strap

From fabric B, cut:
2 main-bag pieces, for lining

From fabric C, cut:
2 rectangles, 3½" x 9", for center panel
1 tab piece
2 rectangles, 7" x 8½", for pocket

From the fusible interfacing, cut:
4 main-bag pieces, for outer bag and lining
2 rectangles, 2½" x 9", for center panel
1 rectangle, 7" x 8½", for pocket
2 tab pieces
1 strip, 2⅜" x 42", for shoulder strap

From the scraps of fusible fleece, cut:
1 tab piece, trimmed as indicated on pattern
2 squares, 1" x 1", for snap reinforcement

"Hobo Handbag," made with fabrics from the Cuzco collection by Kate Spain for Moda Fabrics

PREPARATION

Fuse the interfacing pieces to the wrong side of the corresponding fabric pieces, centering the shoulder strap and center-panel interfacing on the corresponding fabric pieces. Center the corresponding fleece on the fabric A tab and fuse.

CENTER PANELS

1 | Press ½" to the wrong side along both long edges of each center panel.

2 | With both pieces right side up, center a center panel on one outer-bag piece, matching the top and bottom edges, and pin.

3 | Topstitch ¼" from both long edges of the center panel. Make two. **1**

MAGNETIC SNAP

1 | Choose one outer-bag unit to be the front of the bag. Transfer the snap location from the pattern to the fabric.

2 | Fuse one of the 1" squares of fleece to the wrong side of the unit to reinforce the snap position.

3 | Install the magnetic part of the snap at the position indicated, referring to "Magnetic Snaps."

A slim magnetic snap provides a concealed closure for the tab.

1

Topstitch.

Make 2.

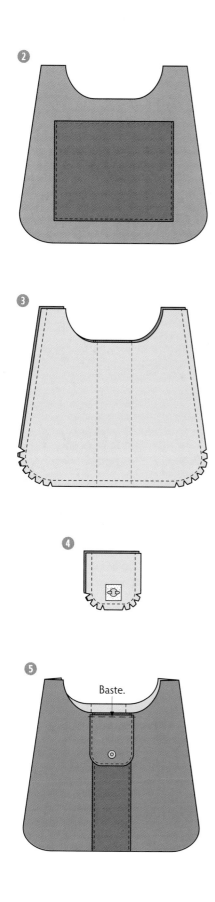

POCKET

1 | Make the pocket, referring to "Lined Patch Pocket."

2 | With both pieces right side up, center the pocket on one lining piece and pin. Stitch ⅛" from the sides and bottom edge of the pocket. **②**

OUTER BAG AND LINING

1 | Pin the outer-bag units right sides together, aligning the edges of the center panel at the bottom edge. Stitch the sides and bottom edge. Notch the curved edges, being careful not to cut the stitching. Press the seam allowances open. **③**

2 | Turn the bag right side out, neatly smoothing the curves and edges into place. Press lightly, using a pressing cloth.

3 | Repeat step 1 to sew the lining pieces together, but leave a 5" gap at the center bottom for turning. Leave the lining wrong side out.

TAB

1 | Transfer the snap location from the pattern to the tab lining. Fuse the second 1" square of fleece to the wrong side of the fabric at the mark. Install the nonmagnetic half of the snap on the tab lining at the marked location, referring to "Magnetic Snaps."

2 | Place the tab pieces right sides together. Stitch the sides and lower edge, leaving the straight edge open. Notch the curved edges. **④**

3 | Turn the tab right side out, using a point turner to smooth the curves, and press. Topstitch ⅛" from the sides and lower edge, leaving the straight edge open.

4 | Center the tab on the back outer bag with right sides together, matching the raw edges and centering the tab on the bag. Baste ¼" from the edge. **⑤**

SHOULDER STRAP

1 | Make the shoulder strap, referring to "Open-Ended Handle."

2 | Pin the ends of the shoulder strap to the right side of the outer bag, centering the strap ends on the side seams and aligning the raw edges. Be sure that the strap is not twisted and baste ¼" from the raw edges. **6**

HOLD THAT POSITION

Pin a few inches of the strap to the bag at both ends, along the outer bag's side seams. This keeps the strap away from the raw edges of the outer bag so that it won't be caught in the stitching during the main assembly.

BAG ASSEMBLY

1 | Insert the outer bag into the lining, right sides together, matching the side seams and aligning the top edges. Pin. Be sure the tab and shoulder strap remain tucked out of the way between the layers.

2 | Stitch around the top edge. Clip the curves and trim across the corners at both sides of the bag, being careful not to cut the stitching. **7**

3 | Turn the bag and lining right side out through the gap in the lining seam. Gently pull on the shoulder strap to help shape the sides and corners. Press the seam allowances to the wrong side along the gap in the lining and pin. Stitch the gap closed, either by hand or with machine stitches placed close to the pressed edges.

4 | Tuck the lining into the outer bag and smooth into place. Press the top edges of the bag so that the seam sits neatly at the top, pressing the tab and shoulder straps away from the bag. Topstitch ¼" from the upper edge around the bag opening. **8**

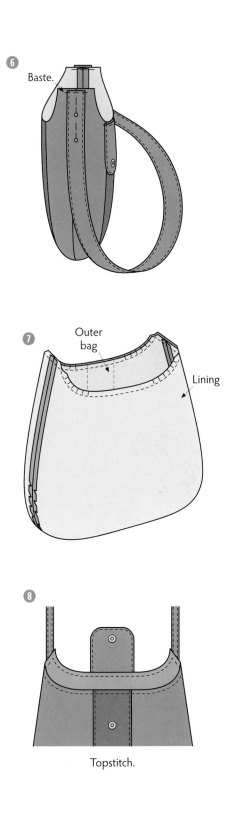

Baste.

Outer bag

Lining

Topstitch.

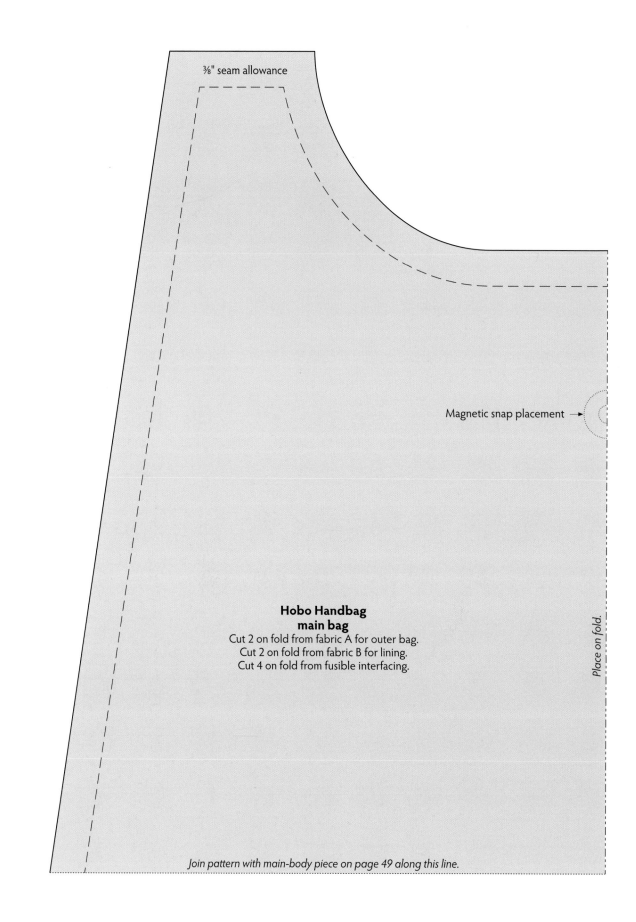

⅜" seam allowance

Magnetic snap placement →

Hobo Handbag
main bag
Cut 2 on fold from fabric A for outer bag.
Cut 2 on fold from fabric B for lining.
Cut 4 on fold from fusible interfacing.

Place on fold.

Join pattern with main-body piece on page 49 along this line.

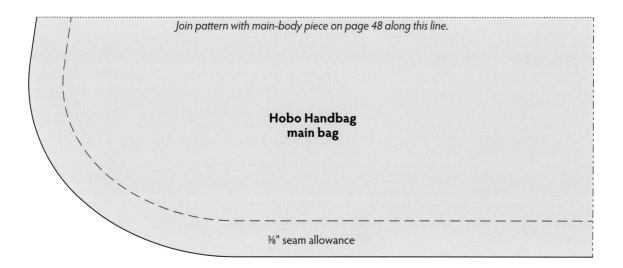

Join pattern with main-body piece on page 48 along this line.

**Hobo Handbag
main bag**

⅜" seam allowance

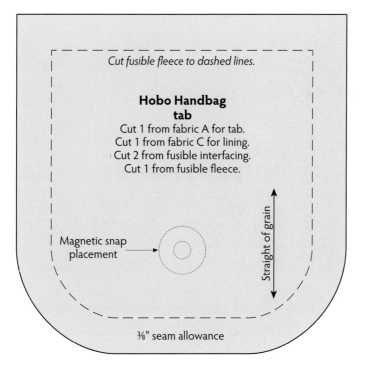

Cut fusible fleece to dashed lines.

**Hobo Handbag
tab**
Cut 1 from fabric A for tab.
Cut 1 from fabric C for lining.
Cut 2 from fusible interfacing.
Cut 1 from fusible fleece.

Straight of grain

Magnetic snap
placement

⅜" seam allowance

TRENDY HIPSTER BAG

Students are sure to love a trendy book bag in modern fabrics. Mix and match black prints with splashes of vivid color for an eye-catching combo.

SKILL LEVEL: Intermediate

FINISHED BAG SIZE: approximately 13¼" x 14" x 4"

TECHNIQUES:

- Bordered Sew-In Pocket (page 14)
- Bordered Patch Pocket (page 14)
- Boxed Bag Base (page 14)
- Open-Ended Handle (page 15)
- Closed-End Handle (page 16)
- Riveted Snaps (page 16)

MATERIALS

Yardage is based on 42"-wide fabric and 20"-wide interfacing.

⅜ yard of fabric A for outer bag and interior pocket

¼ yard of fabric B for lower panels

⅜ yard of fabric C for exterior pocket and shoulder strap

¼ yard of fabric D for tabs and top bands

⅜ yard of fabric E for exterior pocket lining

½ yard of fabric F for bag lining and interior pocket lining

2 yards of fusible nonwoven interfacing (Pellon ES114)*

Two 1" metal D-rings

Two 1" metal swivel hooks

One ⅝" riveted snap

If you use a 35½"-wide interfacing such as Vilene F220, purchase 1¼ yards.

CUTTING

From fabric A, cut:
2 rectangles, 9" x 14", for outer bag
1 square, 9" x 9", for interior pocket

From fabric B, cut:
2 rectangles, 6" x 14", for lower panels

From fabric C, cut:
1 rectangle, 7" x 14", for exterior pocket
1 strip, 4" x 39", for shoulder strap

From fabric D, cut:
1 rectangle, 4" x 5½", for tabs
4 rectangles, 3" x 14", for top bands

From fabric E, cut:
1 rectangle, 9" x 14", for exterior pocket lining

From fabric F, cut:
2 squares, 14" x 14", for lining
1 rectangle, 9" x 11", for interior pocket lining

Continued on page 52

"Trendy Hipster Bag," made with fabric from the Comma collection by Brigitte Heitland for Zen Chic, for Moda Fabrics

Boxed corners give the bag a flat base for plenty of depth.

Continued from page 50

From the fusible interfacing, cut:
2 rectangles, 9" x 14", for outer bag
2 rectangles, 6" x 14", for lower panels
2 squares, 14" x 14", for lining
1 rectangle, 7" x 14", for exterior pocket
1 square, 9" x 9", for interior pocket
1 strip, 2" x 35", for shoulder strap
4 rectangles, 3" x 14", for top bands

GOOD TO KNOW

- All seam allowances are included in the cutting instructions.
- Seam allowances are ⅜" throughout, unless stated otherwise.
- It's a good idea to label each piece as you cut, to avoid any confusion.

PREPARATION

Fuse the interfacing pieces to the wrong side of the corresponding fabric pieces. Center the shoulder strap piece on the fabric, leaving 2" free at each short end, and fuse.

EXTERIOR POCKET

1 | Make the exterior pocket, referring to "Bordered Sew-In Pocket."

2 | Place the pocket on top of one outer-bag pieces, with both pieces right side up, matching the bottom and side edges. Pin. Baste ¼" from the raw edges.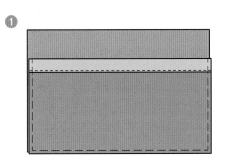

Baste.

OUTER BAG

1 | Sew the top edge of a lower panel to the bottom edge of an outer-bag piece. If you are using a directional print, be sure the design will be correctly oriented when the pieces are assembled. Press the seam allowances toward the lower panels. Topstitch the lower panels, ¼" from the seam. Make two, one with the external pocket in place.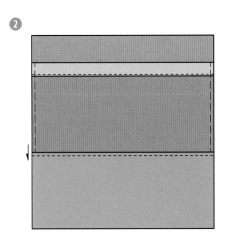

2 │ Sew a top band to the upper edge of each unit. Sew the remaining top bands to the lining pieces. Press the seam allowances toward the top bands. Topstitch the top bands, ¼" from the seam. ❸

INTERIOR POCKET

1 │ Make the interior pocket, referring to "Bordered Patch Pocket."

2 │ With both pieces right side up, center and pin the pocket on one lining piece. Stitch ⅛" from the sides and bottom edge of the pocket. ❹

OUTER BAG AND LINING

1 │ Place the outer-bag pieces right sides together, matching the horizontal seams, and pin.

2 │ Stitch the sides and bottom edge. Press the seam allowances open. Leave the bag wrong side out.

3 │ Repeat steps 1 and 2 to stitch the lining units together, but leave a 6" gap at the center bottom for turning.

4 │ Box the corners of the outer bag and lining to create a depth of 4", referring to "Boxed Bag Base." Turn the outer bag right side out, but leave the lining wrong side out.

TABS

1 │ Prepare the D-ring tab piece, referring to "Open-Ended Handle." Cut the prepared strip in half widthwise to make two tabs of equal size.

2 │ Thread a tab through a D-ring and fold it in half with the D-ring at the fold. Pin the short edges together and baste ¼" from the raw edges. Make two. ❺

3 │ Pin the D-ring tabs to the outer bag, aligning the raw edges and centering each tab over a side seam. Baste ¼" from the raw edges. ❻

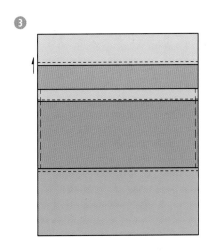

❸

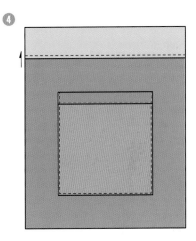

❹

Make 2.

❺

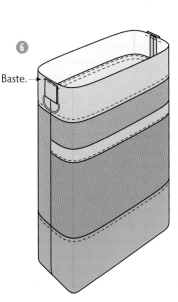

Baste.

❻

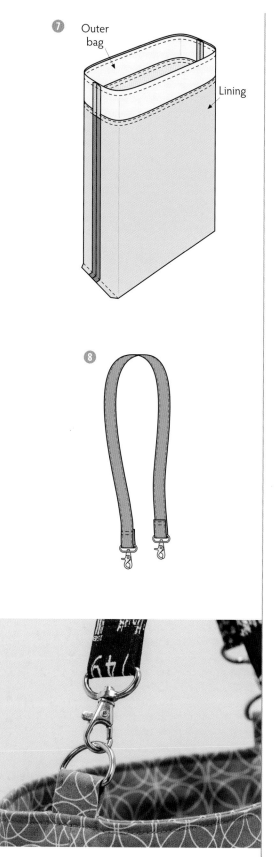

7 Outer bag

Lining

8

Use silver metal D-rings and swivel hooks for a professional finish.

BAG ASSEMBLY

1 | Insert the outer bag into the lining, right sides together, matching the side seams and aligning the top edges. Pin. Be sure the D-ring tabs are tucked out of the way between the layers. Stitch around the top edge. **7**

2 | Turn the bag and lining right side out through the gap in the lining seam. Press both sections lightly, using a pressing cloth. Press the seam allowances along the gap to the wrong side and pin. Stitch the gap closed, either by hand or with machine stitches placed close to the pressed edges.

3 | Tuck the lining inside the bag and smooth it into place. Press the top edges so that the seam sits neatly at the top, pressing the tabs away from the bag. Topstitch ¼" from the edge around the bag opening.

SHOULDER STRAP

1 | Make the shoulder strap, referring to "Closed-End Handle."

2 | Thread one strap end through a swivel hook and fold 1½" of the strap to the wrong side, with the hardware at the fold; pin. Stitch two parallel lines ¼" apart near the end of the strap to secure. Repeat to attach the second swivel hook to the other end of the strap. **8**

3 | Snap the hooks onto the D-rings.

SNAP

Attach the snap parts to the front and back top bands of the bag, positioning them at the center of the bag. Refer to "Riveted Snaps."